© Aladdin Books Ltd 1989

Designed and produced by
Aladdin Books Ltd
70 Old Compton Street
London W1

Design   David West
             Children's Book Design
Editorial Planning   Clark Robinson Limited
Editor   Bibby Whittaker
Researcher   Cecilia Weston-Baker
Illustrated by   Ron Hayward Associates
             and Simon Bishop

EDITORIAL PANEL
The author, Hugh Johnstone,
is an engineer and
science writer who
specializes in transport.

The educational consultant, Peter
Thwaites, is Head of Geography at
Windlesham House School in
Sussex.

The editorial consultant, John Clark,
has contributed to many
information and reference books.

First published in the
United States in 1989 by
Gloucester Press
387 Park Avenue South
New York, NY 10016

Printed in Belgium

Library of Congress Cataloging-in-Publication Data

Johnstone, Hugh
      Aircraft and rockets/ by Hugh Johnstone.
         p. cm. -- (Today's world)
      Includes Index.
      Summary: Describes, in text and illustrations, the characteristics
and functions of a variety of aircraft from the first biplanes and
triplanes to the space shuttles and space explorers such as Voyager.
      ISBN 0-531-17185-X
      1. Airplanes--Juvenile literature. 2. Rockets (Aeronautics)-
-Juvenile literature. [1. Airplanes. 2. Rockets (Aeronautics)]
I. Title. II. Series.
TL547.J57 1989
629.133'34--cd20   89-31583
                                                               CIP
                                                               AC

AIRCRAFT AND SPACE ROCKETS

HUGH JOHNSTONE

GLOUCESTER PRESS
New York · London · Toronto · Sydney

CONTENTS

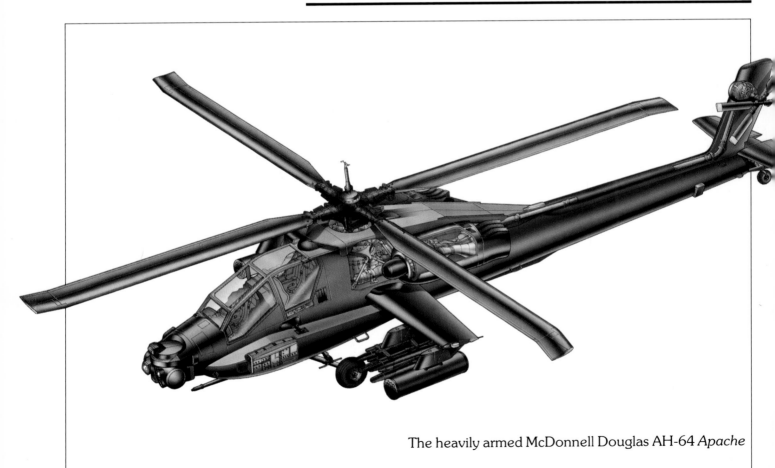

The heavily armed McDonnell Douglas AH-64 *Apache*

The front cover photograph shows the Space Shuttle *Columbia.*

INTRODUCTION

Orville and Wilbur Wright made their historic first flight in 1903 and, after a hesitant start, aviation developed into one of the world's major industries. Progress was very rapid – just 50 years after the first flight, jet aircraft were operating scheduled passenger services at speeds of more than 800 km/h (500 mph) and military aircraft had broken the sound barrier. Air travel has now firmly established itself as the main means of long- distance travel, with more than one billion passenger flights being made each year.

The exploration of space has been equally dramatic. From the launch of the Soviet *Sputnik* in 1957 it took only four years to the first manned space flight, and eight years later American astronaut Neil Armstrong took his dramatic first step onto the Moon's surface. In 1981 the first U.S. Space Shuttle was launched. It was the world's first reusable spacecraft. Despite the disastrous loss of the *Challenger*, the program has resumed successfully. Weather, surveillance, broadcasting and communication satellites are regularly put into orbit by rockets and shuttles, and have a direct and daily effect on our lives.

Half aircraft, half rocket – the NASA Shuttle glides in to land.

The aircraft produced in greatest numbers was the Douglas DC3 *(Dakota)*. In all nearly 11,000 civil and military versions were built.

The specially built *Voyager* aircraft flew around the world non stop in 1986, taking 9 days 3 min 44 sec.

It is less than 90 years since the first powered flight, and in that time aircraft have developed into various different types to suit them to different tasks, civil and military. Most people's flying experiences are with passenger airliners, but these are only a part of civil aviation. Cargo services often follow the same routes as passenger operations, and commonly use freight versions of the same aircraft. Other working aircraft include mail planes, crop sprayers and police surveillance helicopters. Pleasure and sport aircraft include gliders and microlights together with lighter than air balloons. Military aircraft are even more specialized, from fast and maneuverable interceptors to low-flying and hardhitting ground attack aircraft and missile-carrying bombers.

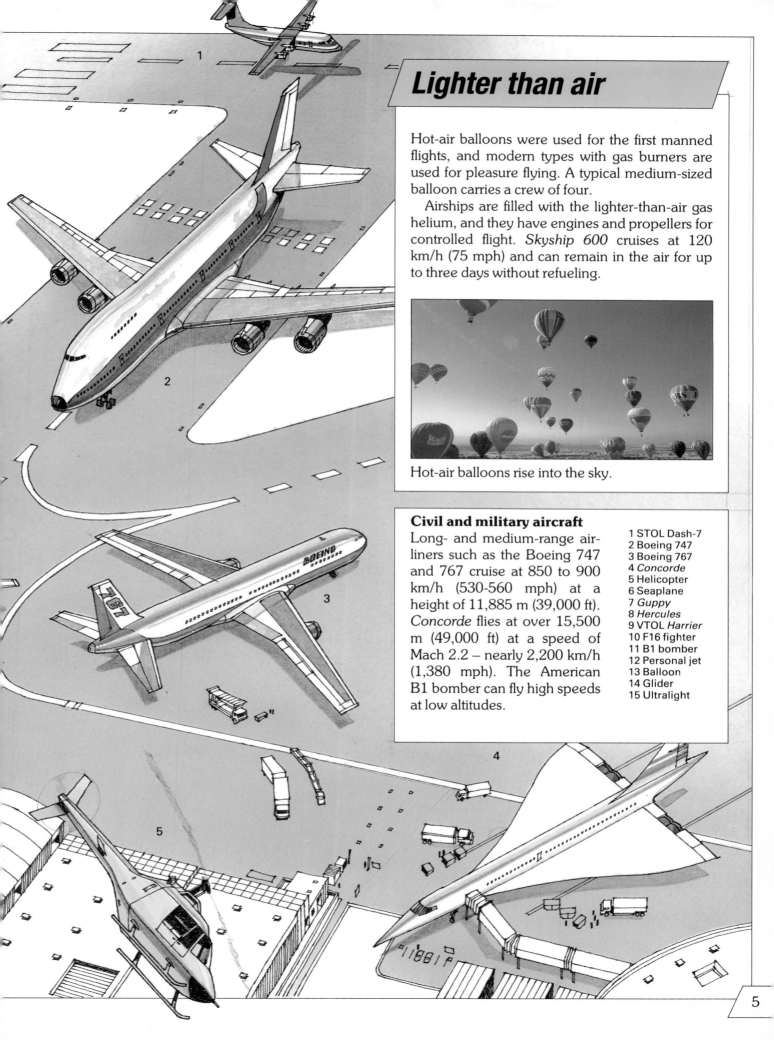

Lighter than air

Hot-air balloons were used for the first manned flights, and modern types with gas burners are used for pleasure flying. A typical medium-sized balloon carries a crew of four.

Airships are filled with the lighter-than-air gas helium, and they have engines and propellers for controlled flight. *Skyship 600* cruises at 120 km/h (75 mph) and can remain in the air for up to three days without refueling.

Hot-air balloons rise into the sky.

Civil and military aircraft

Long- and medium-range airliners such as the Boeing 747 and 767 cruise at 850 to 900 km/h (530-560 mph) at a height of 11,885 m (39,000 ft). *Concorde* flies at over 15,500 m (49,000 ft) at a speed of Mach 2.2 – nearly 2,200 km/h (1,380 mph). The American B1 bomber can fly high speeds at low altitudes.

1 STOL Dash-7
2 Boeing 747
3 Boeing 767
4 *Concorde*
5 Helicopter
6 Seaplane
7 *Guppy*
8 *Hercules*
9 VTOL *Harrier*
10 F16 fighter
11 B1 bomber
12 Personal jet
13 Balloon
14 Glider
15 Ultralight

FLYING IN AIR

The first controlled, powered flight was by the Wright brothers in 1903. Control of the Wright *Flyer* was achieved by twisting the wings.

The Hughes *H4 Hercules* flying boat had a wingspan of 97.5 m (320 ft).

Aircraft are supported in the air by the lift produced by their wings. But successful flight also involves controlling the way the aircraft moves through the air. This is done by moving control surfaces to deflect the airflow and cause the aircraft to alter its position. These surfaces are on the wings and tail unit, and are worked by the pilot's control column, or joystick, and rudder pedals. Normally the controls are directly connected to motors called actuators, which move the control surfaces. In some modern civil and military aircraft fly-by-wire has replaced this system.

Principles of flight

Wings have an airfoil shape which causes the air flowing over the top of the wing to move faster than the air flowing underneath. Where the air moves faster it becomes stretched out and a low pressure area is formed. Pressure under the wing is higher, and this pressure difference produces the lift.

Lift depends on the shape of the wing, the speed of the air and the angle the wing makes with the airflow (the angle of attack). Increasing the angle of attack increases the airflow deflection and gives more lift. With too great an attack angle, or at low air speeds, the airflow breaks away, and lift is lost and the wing stalls.

Increased slow-speed lift, for take-off and landing, is produced by flaps that make the wing wider and more deeply curved.

Control lines that work an airliner's flaps

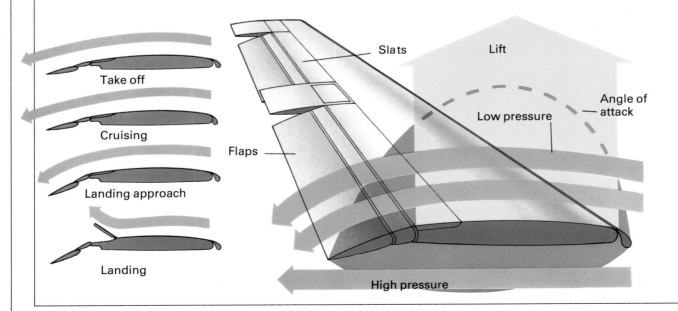

Take off

Cruising

Landing approach

Landing

Slats

Flaps

Lift

Low pressure

Angle of attack

High pressure

The controls

Tailplane elevators produce pitching movements. Pushing the aircraft's control column forward makes the elevators hinge down. This increases their angle of attack so that they generate more lift and force the tail up. Backward column movement has the reverse effect.

Ailerons on the wings move in opposite directions when the control column is operated. One goes up to reduce the lift on the wing at one side, and the other goes down to increase the lift on the other side, giving roll. Turns are made by rolling the aircraft. This directs part of the wing lift away from the vertical, giving a horizontal component that pulls the aircraft round. It also makes the aircraft yaw, and this is corrected by operating the rudder in the direction of the turn.

Up or down
Tail wings turn up to push tail down and nose up.

Turning
Ailerons on right down. Ailerons on left up. Tail fin turns left to correct for yaw.

Flying level
All control surfaces flat unless compensating for crosswind and minor corrections.

Fly-by-wire

Computer technology has led to rapid and radical changes in design. Fly-by-wire was developed initially for combat aircraft, but the latest airliners, including the A320 Airbus, also use electronic fly-by-wire systems. The column is replaced by a one-hand controller mounted to the side of the pilot's seat.

Operation of the controls sends a signal to two different flight management computers. These check the movements the pilot wants and then send signals to actuators that work the control surfaces. If the pilot tries to make a movement that would be unsafe – such as turning too sharply – the control computer will not carry out the order.

A one-handed controller replaces the joystick.

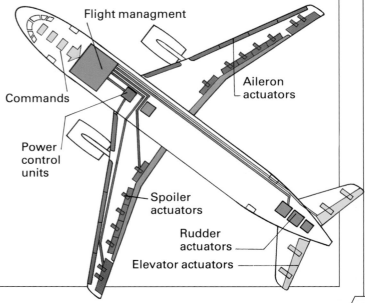

Flight managment

Commands

Power control units

Spoiler actuators

Aileron actuators

Rudder actuators

Elevator actuators

The wings of the Lockheed F104 *Starfighter* are only 10 cm (4 in) thick.

The wing tanks of the A300 *Airbus* can carry nearly 63,000 liters (17,000 gals) of fuel.

The man-powered *Daedalus* has a wingspan of 34m (111ft).

The function of an aircraft's wing is to produce lift. But as it produces lift, it also generates induced drag, which uses up engine power. For this reason, aircraft designers have produced a range of different wing shapes to suit specific applications. In civil airliners the wings contain the fuel tanks, leaving the fuselage free for passengers and cargo.

In a helicopter, lift is produced by the rotor blades which are, in effect, rotating wings powered by the engine. Other forms of lift include the *Harrier* jet's vectored thrust and the tilt-rotor aircraft under development.

Types of wing

The shape of an aircraft's wing is chosen mainly to suit how fast it has to fly. Long narrow wings give good lift and low drag, but have to be strongly made to carry the loads. They are used on gliders and on high-altitude reconnaissance planes. Most airliners have swept-back wings for high cruising speeds, with large flaps to increase the wing area at slower take-off and landing speeds. But they still need long runways.

Swing wings are an effective compromise used for military applications. The wings are swept forward for slow-speed flight, and back for high speeds.

Delta wings are often used for supersonic flight. They have the advantages of swept-back wings but are stronger. They often do not need tailplanes. Wings for supersonic aircraft may be very thin to minimize drag.

When the airflow over a wing reaches the speed of sound – Mach 1 – a shock wave is produced. This occurs before the aircraft reaches the speed of sound, and sweeping the wings back delays the onset of shock.

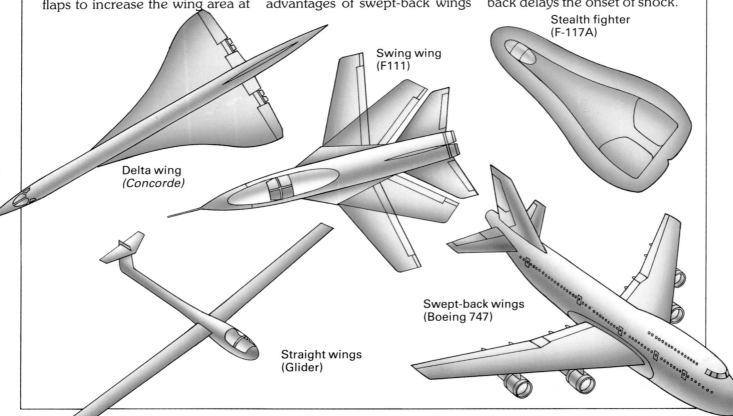

Delta wing
(*Concorde*)

Swing wing
(F111)

Stealth fighter
(F-117A)

Straight wings
(Glider)

Swept-back wings
(Boeing 747)

Rotating wing

Helicopter rotors have long thin blades with an airfoil section. As the rotor turns, the blades move through the air and produce lift to pull the aircraft up into the air. Tilting the rotor makes the helicopter go forward, backward or sideways. Helicopter rotors are driven by an engine so they can take off vertically and hover. If the engine fails the helicopter starts to fall through the air and the resulting airflow makes the rotor turn on its own. Lift is still generated and the pilot can glide the helicopter to a controlled landing. Autogyros have unpowered rotors and an engine that drives a separate propeller. For take-off, power is applied so the autogyro starts to taxi forward. The movement makes the rotor turn, rapidly producing lift to make the autogyro rise into the air after a short run.

An autogyro's rotor is unpowered.

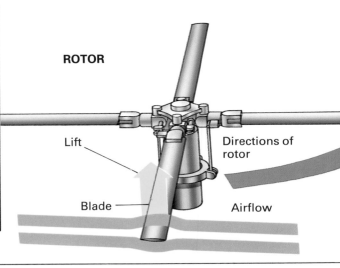

ROTOR

Lift

Directions of rotor

Blade

Airflow

Vertical take-off

Jet engine thrust can be used directly for vertical take-off and landing. In the *Harrier* jump jet the 21,500 lb thrust of the engine is directed through a set of four nozzles, two on each side of the main body.

For take-off the nozzles are swivelled to make the jets point downward, and the jet thrust lifts the aircraft up. Once in the air the pilot gradually turns the nozzles so they point backward. The *Harrier* then flies like a normal aircraft with its wings producing lift.

The nozzles can also be turned to give lift during flight so that the aircraft can fly very slowly, hover, and even move backward.

This aircraft's propellers can be tilted to give vertical lift.

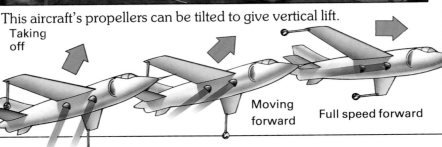

Taking off

Moving forward

Full speed forward

CIVIL AIRCRAFT

The Boeing 307 of 1940 was the first airliner with a fully pressurized passenger cabin.

Comet 1, the first jet airliner, entered service in 1952.

In 1956, American Airlines' passenger milages first exceeded those for the railways.

Civil aircraft range from small air taxis, carrying from four passengers on commuter services of up to 200 miles, to huge subsonic jumbo jets that take more than 600 passengers on short trips, or can cover 9,700 km (6,000 miles) in one flight. There are also supersonic airliners like *Concorde*. With new aircraft, the designers try to achieve the best possible balance between first cost, reliability and operating costs. Weight is restricted wherever possible – on a typical airliner each additional kilogram of structural weight is calculated to use an extra 150 liters (40 gals) of fuel per year.

Modern passenger plane

The internal layout of a passenger airliner depends on the type of service it is being used for. For short-distance commuter or charter applications, the seats are packed close together to carry as many passengers as possible. Where longer, intercontinental journeys are undertaken, the passengers are allowed more space to increase their comfort. For example, the A300 Airbus can carry 345 passengers in a nine-abreast layout with the seats 76 cm (30 in) apart; 285 passengers at a 86 cm (34 in) spacing; and 267 in a mixed class layout. Luggage and cargo are carried under the passenger deck – the A300 cargo holds have a capacity of 147.4 cubic meters (5,205 cubic ft).

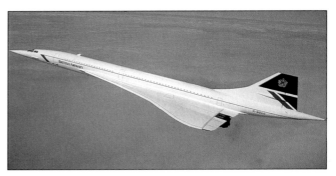

Concorde can fly faster than sound.

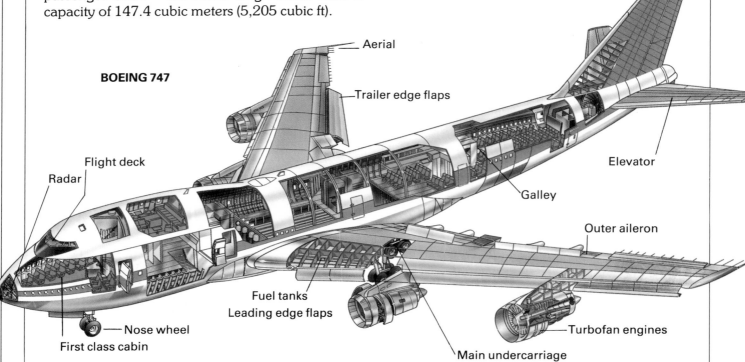

BOEING 747

Aerial
Trailer edge flaps
Flight deck
Radar
Elevator
Galley
Outer aileron
Fuel tanks
Leading edge flaps
Nose wheel
First class cabin
Main undercarriage
Turbofan engines

Civil aircraft variations

Airliners are designed for specific journey types: short-range is up to 1,600km (1,000 miles), mid-range to 4,830km (3,000 miles) and long-range 9,700km (6,000 miles) or more.

Engine positions also vary. Passenger aircraft used for overseas flights that take them more than 90 minutes flying time from land normally have at least three engines to guard against engine failure. However, modern turbofans are very reliable and twin-engined aircraft are starting to be used for such flights.

Mounting the engines on or under the wings causes their weight to act directly against lift, allowing lighter wing structures to be used. The DC9 and Fokker 100 have twin engines at the rear while the Boeing 727 and DC10 have three at the back.

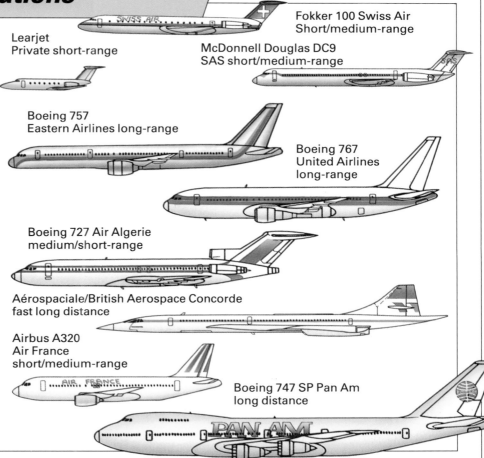

Fokker 100 Swiss Air
Short/medium-range

Learjet
Private short-range

McDonnell Douglas DC9
SAS short/medium-range

Boeing 757
Eastern Airlines long-range

Boeing 767
United Airlines
long-range

Boeing 727 Air Algerie
medium/short-range

Aérospaciale/British Aerospace Concorde
fast long distance

Airbus A320
Air France
short/medium-range

Boeing 747 SP Pan Am
long distance

Cargo

Many cargo aircraft are variations on passenger airliners, with the main differences being the addition of large cargo doors. Heavy transports such as the Antonov and Lockheed C5A *Galaxy* have tail ramps and upward-hinging nose sections. The AN-124 has a main cargo hold that can carry up to 171 tons.

The AN-124 is the world's largest aircraft.

STOL

High-lift wings with multiple flaps and slats are used in short take-off and landing (STOL) aircraft. They can operate from small airfields, including those built close to city centers. One of the most successful designs is the de Havilland Canada *Dash 7*, which carries 50 passengers and can take off in 689 m (2,260 ft).

The *Dash 7* needs only short runways.

GLIDERS AND MICROLIGHTS

Sir George Cayley's glider carried his coachman 457 m (500 yards) in 1853 for the first manned unpowered flight.

The Rogallo kite-wing used for hang gliders was developed by NASA for the recovery of space capsules.

Early aviators learned how to fly using gliders. Modern competition gliders use advanced aerodynamics and high-technology materials to obtain maximum performance. For launching, gliders are pulled along on a cable or towed up by a powered aircraft. The altitude record for a glider is 14,938m (49,009 ft).

Hang gliding is the simplest form of flying. The pilot is suspended beneath a kite-like aerofoil and controls the flight by moving his body around. Most flights are made using the upward air currents produced by wind blowing up a hill.

Gliders

The high-performance competition glider and World championship winner, Schemp-Hirth *Discus K*, has a 15 m (49 ft) wingspan and an empty weight of 228 kg (503 lb). Maximum speed in still air is 250 km/h (155 mph) and the glide ratio is 42.2 – it flies along for 42.2 m for each metre it sinks (in the absence of an updraught).

After launching, glider flights are sustained using hill lift or patches of rising warm air known as thermals. The pilot flies around in the thermal and is carried up by the rising air. When sufficient height has been gained, the pilot flies out of the thermal across country, searching for new thermals as height is lost.

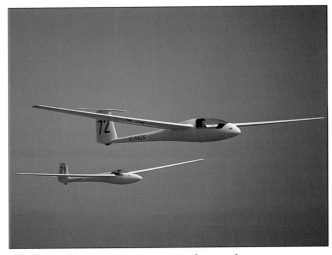

Gliders climb using warm-air thermals.

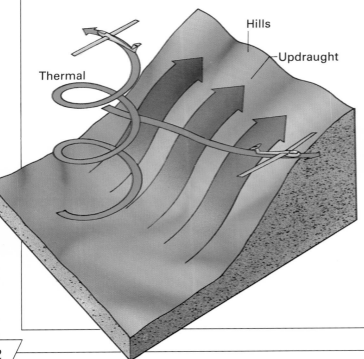

Thermal

Hills

Updraught

A hang glider is a man-carrying kite.

Microlight aircraft

Microlights are powered aircraft with an empty weight not greater than 150 kg (330 lb). They can be flown without the pilot having to obtain a full pilot's licence. In the United States they are called ultralights, and the weight limit is 115 kg (254 lb).

The simplest designs are basically motorized hang gliders. The pilot rides in a seat and controls the aircraft by shifting his body weight. More elaborate designs include monoplanes with a light alloy wing structure covered in a fabric such as dacron. They use a control column and rudder pedals like a conventional aircraft, and may even have enclosed cockpits. A typical microlight has a wingspan of 10 m (33 ft) and a length of 5 m (16 ft), with an empty weight of around 110 kg (245 lb). A 28hp engine drives a 1.22 m (4 ft) light propeller to give a maximum level speed of just over 90 km/h (55 mph).

A microlight is the simplest powered aircraft.

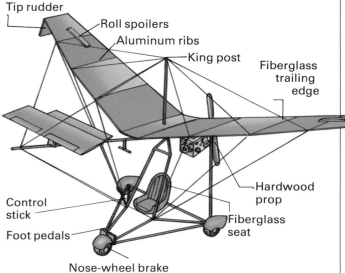

Tip rudder
Roll spoilers
Aluminum ribs
King post
Fiberglass trailing edge
Hardwood prop
Fiberglass seat
Control stick
Foot pedals
Nose-wheel brake

Aircraft for pleasure

Aerobatic aircraft are strongly constructed to take the high stresses created by the maneuvers. Most are biplanes (with two pairs of wings), which can make tight turns.

There are many enthusiasts who fly and even build their own aircraft. Kits containing critical components and plans for many homebuilt designs, including helicopters, are readily available. These aircraft are often sophisticated designs offering flying speeds of over 250 km/h (155 mph). Before they can be flown, they have to be examined and given an airworthiness certificate.

A typical monoplane used for pleasure

MILITARY AIRCRAFT

The first operational turbojet was the twin-engined Messer-schmidt Me262 in 1944.

F100 *Super Sabres* were the first fighters to break the sound barrier in level flight.

Versions of the Soviet Mig25 can fly at Mach 3.2.

Military aircraft make use of the very latest in aerospace technology. Advanced manufacturing techniques and materials are employed to give the best possible performance. The main goals are to produce a tough and reliable aircraft which can perform its designated role, while carrying the latest weapons.

Systems and techniques developed for military purposes are often applied to later generations of civil aircraft. Recent examples include the use of weight-saving composite materials and electronic fly-by-wire controls.

Multi-role aircraft

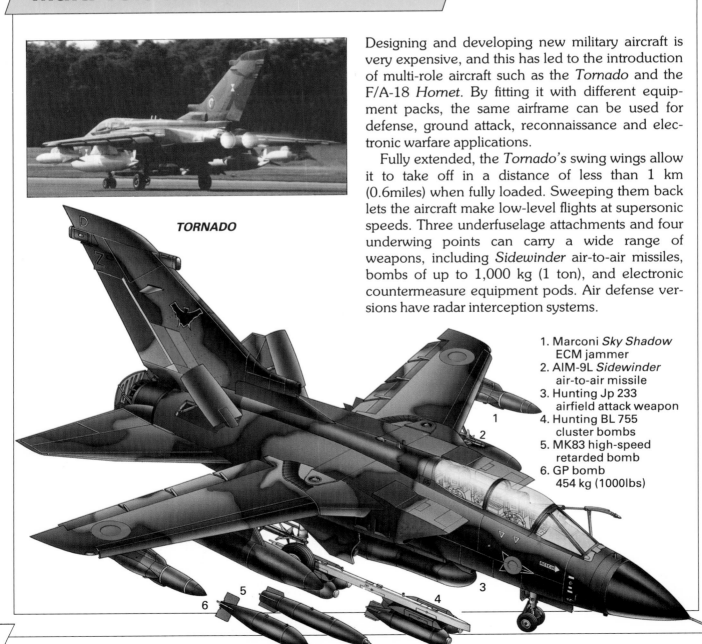

TORNADO

Designing and developing new military aircraft is very expensive, and this has led to the introduction of multi-role aircraft such as the *Tornado* and the F/A-18 *Hornet*. By fitting it with different equipment packs, the same airframe can be used for defense, ground attack, reconnaissance and electronic warfare applications.

Fully extended, the *Tornado's* swing wings allow it to take off in a distance of less than 1 km (0.6miles) when fully loaded. Sweeping them back lets the aircraft make low-level flights at supersonic speeds. Three underfuselage attachments and four underwing points can carry a wide range of weapons, including *Sidewinder* air-to-air missiles, bombs of up to 1,000 kg (1 ton), and electronic countermeasure equipment pods. Air defense versions have radar interception systems.

1. Marconi *Sky Shadow* ECM jammer
2. AIM-9L *Sidewinder* air-to-air missile
3. Hunting Jp 233 airfield attack weapon
4. Hunting BL 755 cluster bombs
5. MK83 high-speed retarded bomb
6. GP bomb 454 kg (1000lbs)

Craft for different jobs

Some aircraft are designed mainly for one purpose, such as the Mach 2.5 air-superiority F-15 fighter. They can be upgraded to carry out other tasks like ground attack but for maximum ground strike, the *Thunderbolt* is outstanding. Titanium armour for the pilot and damage-resistant construction minimize the effects of ground fire, and the 30 mm cannon firing 70 rounds per second complements a bomb and missile load of up to 7,252 kg (16,000 lb).

Other aircraft such as the close-support jump-jet *Harrier*, the Lockheed SR-71 *Blackbird* and long-range B1 strategic bomber all meet specific military needs. Back-up for these fighting aircraft is supplied by transports like the all purpose *Galaxy* and the KC-10A *Extender*, which carries passengers and cargo as well as fuel for in-flight refueling.

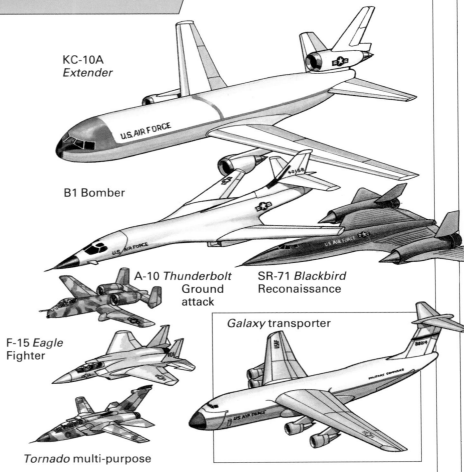

KC-10A *Extender*

B1 Bomber

A-10 *Thunderbolt* Ground attack

SR-71 *Blackbird* Reconaissance

Galaxy transporter

F-15 *Eagle* Fighter

Tornado multi-purpose

Stealth

Stealth aircraft are designed to avoid radar by absorbing or deflecting signals so that they are not reflected back to the radar transmitter. To do this the body and wings are smoothly curved so the signals bounce off to the side. Where possible, materials transparent to radar signals, like composite plastics, are used, and other surfaces are treated with radar-absorbing coatings.

Special attention is paid to the position of the engines, because the rapidly rotating fan blades normally reflect radar signals well. The engines are set well back into the wing or body structure, with long inlet and exhaust ducts to diffuse and absorb radar signals.

Inlet diffuses signal

Signal ricochets off curved surface

Radar beam

Stealth profile

Less radar energy returned

The American F-117A stealth aircraft.

HELICOPTERS

The Italian artist and inventor Leonardo da Vinci designed a helicopter-like lifting screw made of starched linen in 1490.

The Frenchman Paul Cornu made the first free helicopter flight in 1907.

The ability to take off and land vertically on unprepared sites, and to remain hovering over a specific spot, makes helicopters the most versatile aircraft. Initially these advantages were most appreciated by military users, who were also willing to accept the high operating costs of early designs. Intensive development has produced reliable, efficient machines that have many civil applications, including passenger transport and cargo delivery, flying cranes, ambulances, agriculture and police surveillance. The main limitation of helicopters is their slow speed.

Helicopter Blades

Most helicopters have a single main rotor, with a tail rotor to counteract the torque reaction that tends to make the cabin rotate as well. At high flight speeds the advancing blade may be moving at close to the speed of sound. These effects limit maximum speed – the record of 400.87 km/h (249.1 mph) was set by a *Lynx* using special blades with enlarged tips.

Designers are constantly looking for ways to increase speeds. Convertiplanes like the *Osprey* have rotors that can be tilted from the vertical to the horizontal so they act as propellers, with lift being provided by ordinary wings. Although prototypes have flown successfully, they have yet to enter service.

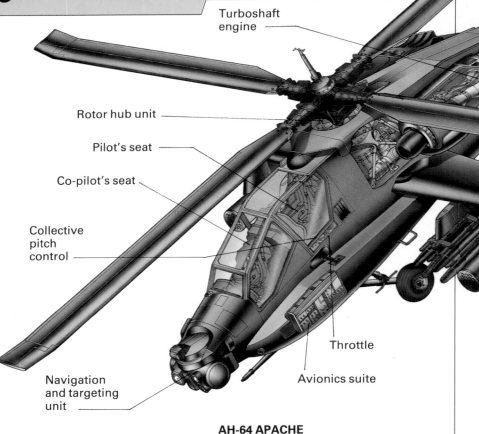

- Turboshaft engine
- Rotor hub unit
- Pilot's seat
- Co-pilot's seat
- Collective pitch control
- Navigation and targeting unit
- Throttle
- Avionics suite

AH-64 APACHE

Helicopter flying near buildings

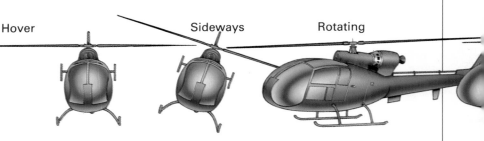

Hover   Sideways   Rotating

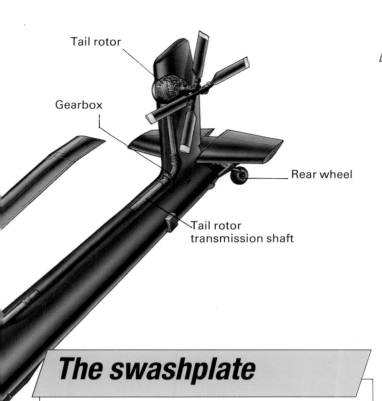

Tail rotor

Gearbox

Rear wheel

Tail rotor transmission shaft

Different types

Sea King helicopters are used for anti-submarine and air-sea rescue operations, with a 200km/h (129 mph) cruising speed and a 1,230 km (764 mile) range. The Sikorsky S.61 is an earlier 30-seat passenger version of the *Sea King*. Twin-rotor *Chinooks* can carry up to 44 passengers, an internal payload of 9,072 kg (20,000 lb) or 12,700 kg (28,000 lb) suspended below the helicopter on a cargo hook.

Military applications remain the major use of helicopters, and the Hughes *Apache* attack helicopter has advanced avionics giving it full day and night capability. The main armament is a 625 rounds per minute 30 mm automatic cannon. It also carries 16 *Hellfire* anti-tank missiles or 76 2.75-in rockets. Maximum level speed is about 300 km/h (190 mph).

Chinook lifter-helicopter

Hughes AH-64 *Apache* attack helicopter

Westland *Sea King* rescue helicopter

Bell 206-B commuter helicopter

Hughes TH-55 *Osage* crop sprayer

Sikorsky S.61 passenger helicopter

The swashplate

Operation of a helicopter's rotor is controlled by a swashplate. Moving the complete swashplate up or down alters the pitch of the rotor blades, and so increases or decreases the lift. When hovering, the pitch of all the blades is the same. To move forward the swashplate is tilted forward, changing the pitch of the blade at each point and dropping the nose of the helicopter. To fly backward the reverse occurs – the swashplate is tilted backward, the pitch of the blades is altered and the nose lifts.

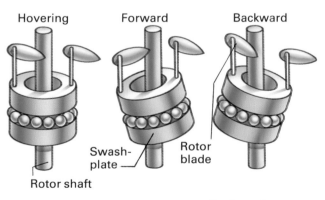

Hovering   Forward   Backward

Swash-plate   Rotor blade

Rotor shaft

Forward   Backward

17

CROWDED SKIES

At Chicago O'Hare airport, the world's busiest, there is an aircraft landing or taking off every 40 seconds on average.

Small aircraft following larger ones are spaced farther apart on their final landing approach to avoid turbulence in the air caused by the larger aircraft.

The tremendous growth in air traffic has resulted in increasing congestion of the airways. Strict air traffic control procedures minimize the risk of collisions occurring and keep the aircraft moving as efficiently as possible.

An aircraft cannot merely take off at any time and fly anywhere. A flight plan of the route is drawn up and approved by the authorities. The aircraft's progress is checked at every stage by air traffic controllers. At peak periods the airspace is overcrowded resulting in considerable delays with aircraft unable to take off.

Navigation

Navigation in controlled airspace generally involves flying along airways marked by VOR (very high frequency omni-directional range) beacons. Away from controlled airspace the simplest form of navigation is dead reckoning. The navigator calculates the aircraft's position from the known starting point and the flight speed, time and direction, making corrections for wind effects.

Airliners generally have inertial navigation systems. These use a set of accelerometers on a gyroscope-stabilized platform to measure the acceleration of the aircraft in all three directions (forward, sideways and up or down). A computer then calculates the position of the aircraft in relation to its starting point.

The *Navstar* navigation system calculates positions using signals from at least four satellites orbiting the Earth. The civil version can establish positions to within 200 m (600 ft), and the military version is accurate to 10 m (30 ft).

1 Weather radar
2 ILS Localizer receiver
3 ILS Glidescope receiver
4 VHF communications aerial
5 Satellite communications aerial
6 Radio altimeters
7 Omega aerial
8 VOR receiver
9 Avionics bay
10 ADF (Automatic Direction Finder) aerial
11 Doppler radar
12 Transponder aerials
13 Marker-beacon receiver
14 LORAN (Long RAnge Navigation Aerial)
15 DME (Distance Measuring Equipment) aerials

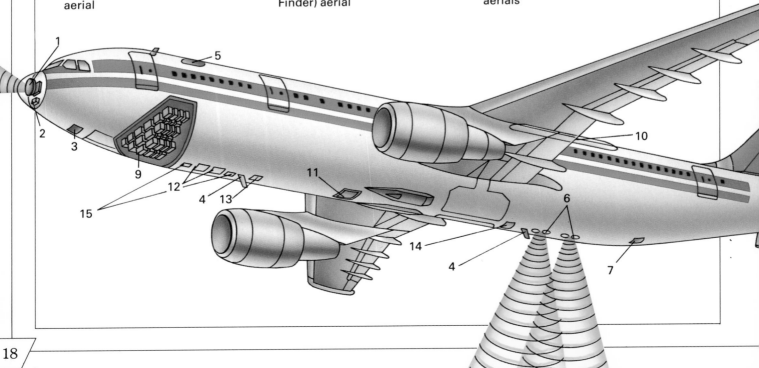

Radar control

Air traffic controllers are responsible for a particular airspace sector, and they use radar screens to track the paths of the aircraft passing through it. Extra information is provided by an aircraft's transponders, which transmit a positive identification signal and a height reading.

Within the sector, the controller tells the pilot the height and speed to fly at and the route to follow. A buildup of arrivals at an airport creates a line of aircraft waiting to land. The controller may direct the pilots to join a stack of aircraft circling at specified heights around a beacon. The aircraft is then moved out of the stack and handed over to the Airport Control Tower, which handles the aircraft's final approach and landing.

Air traffic control radar

Access route

Closely specified path through crowded airspace to take the aircraft to planned cruising height.

VOR navigation beacon

Transmits a continuous radio signal used by aircraft for direction finding.

Radar hand-over point

Responsibility for the aircraft is passed from the airport controller to the next sector.

8

Airport control

Responsible for arrivals, departures and through traffic in the airspace up to 36 km (20 miles) around the airport.

Aircraft movements in busy traffic areas are confined to airways. Aircraft traveling in opposite directions fly at different levels, at least 300 m (1,000 ft) apart. Other aircraft to the sides have to be at least 8 km (5 miles) away and those in front or behind at least 10 minutes flying time away. This is reduced on airport approach.

AIRCRAFT OR SPACE ROCKET?

The first aircraft to fly faster than sound was a Bell X-1.

An SR-71A *Blackbird* flew from New York to London in 1 hour 55 minutes in 1974.

The Lockheed TR-1A reconnaissance aircraft has an operational ceiling of 27,430 m (90,000 ft).

In 1981 the U.S. Space Shuttle blasted off as a rocket and came back to Earth as a glider.

Space is defined as the universe lying beyond the Earth's atmosphere, which extends to an altitude of 100 km (62 miles). Conventional flight at such heights is impossible because the air is too rarefied to provide aerodynamic lift, although special rocket planes can operate in this zone.

Recently there has been considerable interest in developing spaceplanes such as the British Hotol and the American Orient Express. These spaceplanes take off like aircraft and fly right through the atmosphere into space. They could be used to carry payloads into low Earth orbits, or developed for use as intercontinental transports. Speeds of the order of 30,000 km/h (18,500 mph) could be achieved and a spaceplane of this type could fly from London, England, to Sydney, Australia, in around 45 minutes.

Rocket planes

There have been many designs for spacecraft, but first the unknown problem of entering space had to be encountered. American research into supersonic and hypersonic flight was carried out using a series of rocket-powered aircraft. In 1947 American Charles Yeager flew the X-1 rocketplane to break the sound barrier for the first time. These culminated with the X-15A-2, which had a 70,000 lb thrust rocket engine and was launched in the air from beneath a B-52 bomber at 10,670 m (35,000 ft) before firing the engine. On separate flights the aircraft reached an altitude of 107,960 m (354,199 ft), and a maximum speed of 6,692 km/h (4,158 mph).

The high-flying, supersonic Bell X-1 rocket plane

Special engines

Central to the Hotol project are the engines, which can work as turbofans in the atmosphere and as oxygen-hydrogen rockets in space. The change-over would take place at an altitude of around 26,000 m (85,000 ft) and a speed of Mach 5.

HOTOL

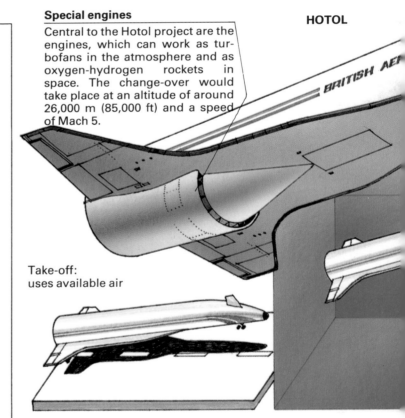

Take-off: uses available air

Hotol: rocket plane of the future

Hotol stands for Horizontal Take-Off and Landing. It is designed to be a fully developed spaceplane that takes off and lands using a normal runway. The heavy fuel load needed means that the take-off weight of 250,000 kg (551,155 lb) would be around five times the landing weight of 47,500 kg (104,719 lb), and a special laser-guided

Conventional rocket

Altitude has a small effect on space rocket thrust because the jet velocity increases as the atmospheric pressure falls. Both the US and USSR developed rockets for their ICBMs (Intercontinental Ballistic Missiles), and used versions to put satellites and men into space. Today's space shuttles rely on rocket power, as does the European Ariane space programme.

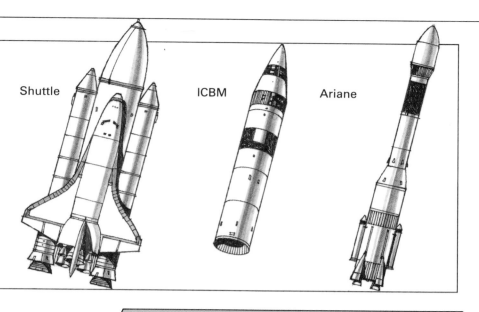

Shuttle   ICBM   Ariane

On the edge of space

High-speed, high-altitude flight imposes enormous strains on aircraft, and one of the most successful designs is the Lockheed SR-71 *Blackbird* reconnaissance aircraft. It has a 16.94 m (55.6 ft) wingspan and a length of 32.7 m (107.4 ft). Take-off weight is 77.1 tons (175,000 lb), around 11 tons (25,000 lb) of which is fuel, giving a range of 4,800 km (2,982 miles). The aircraft does not normally take off fully loaded, however; the fuel load is taken on from a flight refuelling tanker after the aircraft is airborne. The fastest recorded speed for the SR-71 is 3,529.6 km/h (2,193.2 mph) and the maximum height it can achieve is around 30,480 m (100,000 ft).

Shape

Overall length is 63 m (207 ft), with a 28.3 m (93 ft) wingspan and a height of 12.8 m (42 ft). Most of the space is taken up by the fuel tanks: hydrogen at the rear and oxygen at the front. The cargo bay is 7.5 m (24.6 ft) long, with the engine mounted behind it.

Orbit: carries liquid oxygen and fuel

Landing: uses available air

trolley would be used to support the spaceplane for take-off. The built-in undercarriage is used for landing, which needs a 1,500 m (4,925 ft) runway. Hotol is designed for automatic, unmanned operation with later development to a manned craft. It could carry payloads of up to 8,000 kg (17,635 lb) into a 300 km (162 mile) Equatorial Earth Orbit.

The *Blackbird* is used for high-altitude reconnaissance.

SHUTTLES

The weight of the NASA Shuttle external fuel tank was reduced by 270 kg (600 lb) by leaving off the top coat of white paint.

A faulty seal on one of the booster rockets caused the destruction of *Challenger* on the 25th Shuttle flight.

The first Soviet Shuttle, *Buran*, flew on November 15th, 1988.

After a rocket is launched into space, most of the rocket either falls back into the atmosphere and is burned up, or continues into space to become orbiting garbage. This is a wasteful and expensive process and the NASA Space Shuttle was developed to provide a more efficient alternative.

The basic concept is of a reusable spacecraft that is launched with rocket assistance and returns to Earth as a glider. Crew and passengers travel in a pressurized cabin, making it possible to carry specialists such as engineers and scientists without their having to undergo astronaut flight training. Cargo, including satellites, is carried in a separate bay which is large enough to take significant loads into space or bring them back to Earth. In 1984 the shuttle *Discovery* recovered two faulty satellites from orbit and returned them to Earth for repair.

Soviet and American Shuttles

The American Shuttle has its main lift engines in the orbiter, with fuel being carried in a 47 m (154 ft) long external tank which is jettisoned during the launch. Additional launch thrust comes from solid-fuel rocket boosters, which are recovered for reuse. About the size of an airliner, the orbiter is 37 m (122 ft) long with a 24 m (78 ft) wingspan and a weight of 75 tonnes unladen. Most of the structure is aluminium with heat-insulating outer layers, including ceramic tiles for critical areas.

Cargo bay dimensions are 18.3 m (60 ft) long by 4.6 m (15 ft) wide, and loads of up to 29,500 kg (65,000 lb) can be carried into low orbit. One important load is *Spacelab*, which couples up to the crew cabin and lets scientists carry out research experiments.

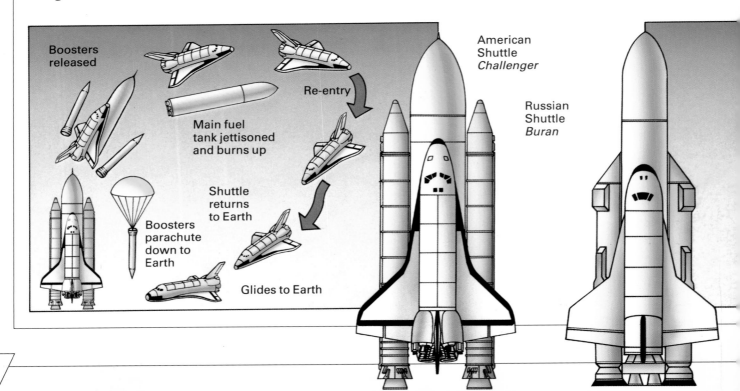

Boosters released

Main fuel tank jettisoned and burns up

Re-entry

Shuttle returns to Earth

Boosters parachute down to Earth

Glides to Earth

American Shuttle *Challenger*

Russian Shuttle *Buran*

Shuttle variants

Hermes is a French design intended for servicing space stations, and is launched by the *Ariane 5* rocket into orbits 400 to 800 km (250 to 500 miles) up. It can carry a crew of three and a payload of up to 3 tons in the 3m (9.8 ft) wide cargo bay. There are twin orbital engines, but *Hermes* is designed to glide down to land after re-entry.

The Japanese also have plans for a four-person shuttle. It will be rocket launched, and the design incorporates a jet engine for use when landing.

The Soviet *Cosmos* spaceplane appears to be complementary to the Soviet shuttle. The probable use is for ferrying astronauts between Earth and the Soviet space stations. The spaceplane could also provide a space rescue service.

Cosmos launch booster

Soviet Mini-shuttle *Cosmos*

The Soviet Shuttle is broadly similar to the American one, because both designs have to work under the same conditions. The major difference is that the Soviet craft has no launch engines; it is carried into space by the *Energia* booster, which is itself recoverable. The orbiter can be operated unmanned and the maneuvering engines give a limited flight ability within the atmosphere.

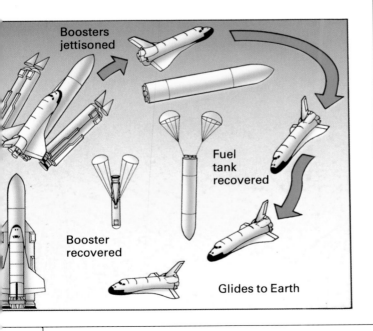

Boosters jettisoned

Fuel tank recovered

Booster recovered

Glides to Earth

Artist's impression of *Hermes*

Saturn V moon rockets were 111 m (364 ft) high when fitted with the Apollo spacecraft.

Sputnik 1, the first satellite, weighed 83.6 kg (184.3 lb).

The *Voyager* probes took more than 3 years to reach Saturn.

Soviet *Energia* rockets with four boosters can lift more than 150 tons to a 200 km (125 mile) orbit.

Rockets are the main way of launching satellites and space probes. Multi-stage arrangements are used to increase the mass that can be carried into space. In a typical three-stage rocket, the third stage carries the payload and delivers it into the final orbit. The first and second stage rockets fire in sequence to give the third stage high speed and altitude before it starts operating. As each stage burns out it is discarded, reducing the mass to be lifted. Added thrust for take-off is obtained from booster rockets that strap on to the first stage. Most of the weight of a launch rocket is fuel; in the Ariane 3 launcher the payload is just 1 percent of the launch weight, and the rocket structure makes up a further 9 percent. During September 1985 there were nearly 6,000 objects in orbit. More than 4,000 of them were debris like rocket casings, protective panels and redundant satellites.

Payloads

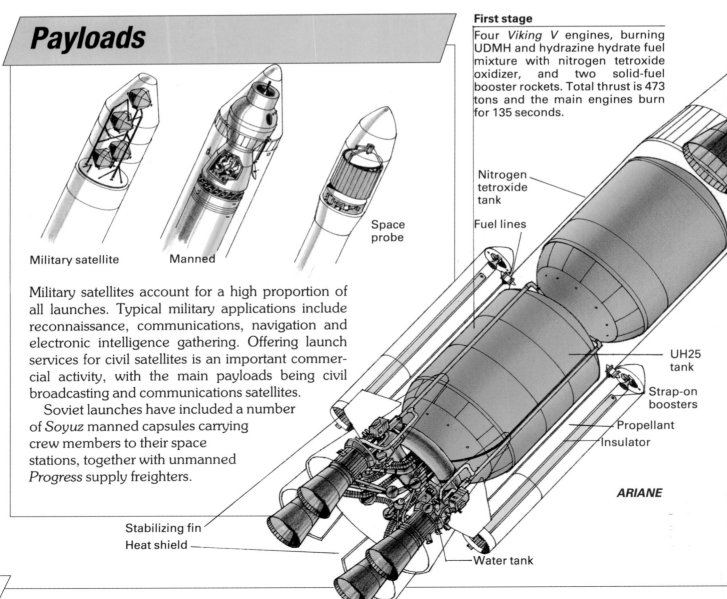

Military satellite

Manned

Space probe

First stage

Four *Viking V* engines, burning UDMH and hydrazine hydrate fuel mixture with nitrogen tetroxide oxidizer, and two solid-fuel booster rockets. Total thrust is 473 tons and the main engines burn for 135 seconds.

Nitrogen tetroxide tank

Fuel lines

UH25 tank

Strap-on boosters

Propellant

Insulator

Stabilizing fin

Heat shield

Water tank

ARIANE

Military satellites account for a high proportion of all launches. Typical military applications include reconnaissance, communications, navigation and electronic intelligence gathering. Offering launch services for civil satellites is an important commercial activity, with the main payloads being civil broadcasting and communications satellites.

Soviet launches have included a number of *Soyuz* manned capsules carrying crew members to their space stations, together with unmanned *Progress* supply freighters.

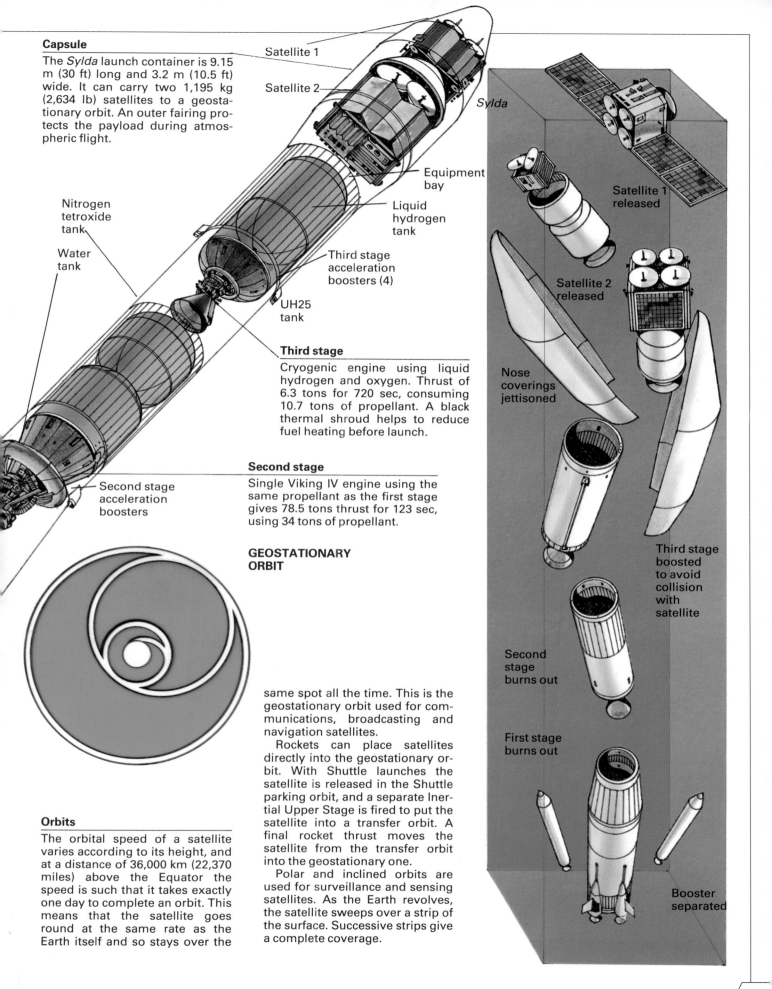

Capsule

The *Sylda* launch container is 9.15 m (30 ft) long and 3.2 m (10.5 ft) wide. It can carry two 1,195 kg (2,634 lb) satellites to a geostationary orbit. An outer fairing protects the payload during atmospheric flight.

Satellite 1

Satellite 2

Sylda

Nitrogen tetroxide tank

Water tank

Equipment bay

Liquid hydrogen tank

Third stage acceleration boosters (4)

UH25 tank

Second stage acceleration boosters

Third stage

Cryogenic engine using liquid hydrogen and oxygen. Thrust of 6.3 tons for 720 sec, consuming 10.7 tons of propellant. A black thermal shroud helps to reduce fuel heating before launch.

Second stage

Single Viking IV engine using the same propellant as the first stage gives 78.5 tons thrust for 123 sec, using 34 tons of propellant.

GEOSTATIONARY ORBIT

Satellite 1 released

Satellite 2 released

Nose coverings jettisoned

Third stage boosted to avoid collision with satellite

Second stage burns out

First stage burns out

Booster separated

Orbits

The orbital speed of a satellite varies according to its height, and at a distance of 36,000 km (22,370 miles) above the Equator the speed is such that it takes exactly one day to complete an orbit. This means that the satellite goes round at the same rate as the Earth itself and so stays over the same spot all the time. This is the geostationary orbit used for communications, broadcasting and navigation satellites.

Rockets can place satellites directly into the geostationary orbit. With Shuttle launches the satellite is released in the Shuttle parking orbit, and a separate Inertial Upper Stage is fired to put the satellite into a transfer orbit. A final rocket thrust moves the satellite from the transfer orbit into the geostationary one.

Polar and inclined orbits are used for surveillance and sensing satellites. As the Earth revolves, the satellite sweeps over a strip of the surface. Successive strips give a complete coverage.

War rockets built by the Englishman Congreve had a range of 4,500 m (15,000 ft). More than 5,000 were used to bombard Copenhagen in 1807.

The German V-1 was a simple cruise missile flying at 900 km/h (560 mph).

Strategic nuclear missiles have an awesome destructive capacity, some carrying warheads with megaton explosive powers. Intercontinental ballistic missiles (ICBMs) have a range of at least 8,000 km (5,000 miles) and reach a height of around 1,600 km (1,000 miles) during their flight.

Antiaircraft and antiship missiles carry high explosive warheads and have engines that operate continuously during the flight; solid fuel rockets are often used. Cruise missiles are unmanned aircraft armed with powerful warheads that fly at low level to avoid detection.

MIRV

A single missile can deliver multiple warheads using the MIRV (multiple independent reentry vehicle) system. The rocket boosts a warhead "bus" into a ballistic trajectory, where a guidance system lets it move away from the original path of the missile. The individual warheads, together with decoys, are released from the bus and re-enter the atmosphere to attack a series of separate targets. The American Peacekeeper (MX) missiles have ten warheads, each with a 500 kiloton yield. The warhead guidance systems ensure that the warheads explode within 40 m (130 ft) of their target.

ICBMs may be launched from mobile road transporters or trains, or held in underground silos to resist attack. Cold launch systems use a separate propellant to blow the missile out of the silo before the engines are fired. This means the silo can be readily reloaded with another missile. A similar system is used to launch missiles from submerged submarines. Submarine-based missiles are hard to detect, but tend to have a reduced accuracy of around 500 m (1,625 ft).

COLD LAUNCH

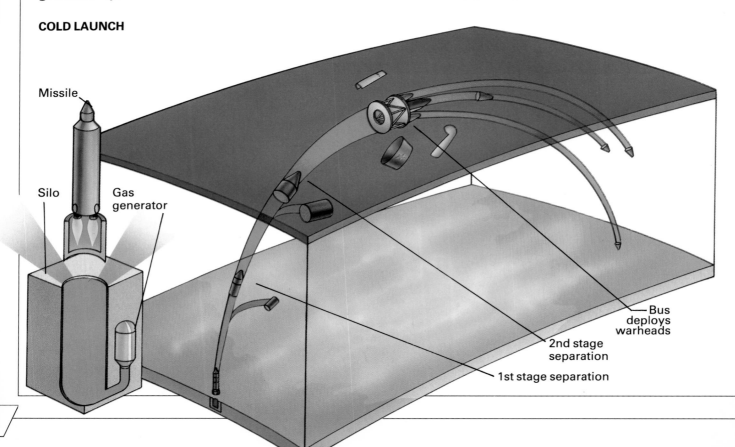

Missile

Silo   Gas generator

Bus deploys warheads

2nd stage separation

1st stage separation

Warhead

Bus

SECOND STAGE

FIRST STAGE

Star Wars

The Strategic Defense Initiative, or Star Wars, is an American program to defend against nuclear missile attack. Flight time for an ICBM is around 25 minutes and the warheads travel at 25,000 km/h (15,000 mph), making them very difficult targets.

The best time to attack the missiles is after the boost stage but before the bus has released the warheads. This phase lasts around 5 minutes and in a full-scale attack several thousand missiles would have to be dealt with. Possible attack systems include satellite battle stations carrying chemical and X ray lasers, rail guns firing small metal slugs at velocities of 100 km/s (60 miles per second) and interceptor missiles.

Destroying the individual warheads is more difficult and needs sophisticated sensors to distinguish between the live warheads and decoys. Laser and missile systems would also be used for this.

An antimissile satellite carries laser weapons.

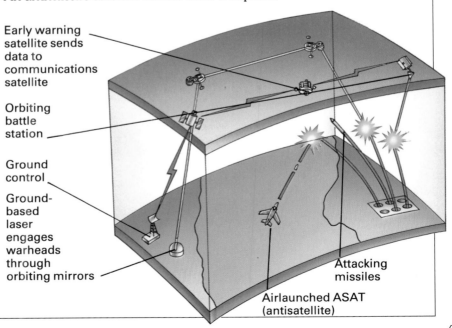

Early warning satellite sends data to communications satellite

Orbiting battle station

Ground control

Ground-based laser engages warheads through orbiting mirrors

Attacking missiles

Airlaunched ASAT (antisatellite)

Soviet cosmonaut Yuri Gagarin's first manned space flight consisted of one orbit, lasting 1hr 48min.

American *Saturn V* Moon rockets carried three astronauts to the Moon, two of whom landed.

Exploration of space is the last great adventure, and it is being carried out in the full public gaze. Millions watched American Neil Armstrong's first step on the Moon – and millions saw the U.S. Shuttle *Challenger* blow up in January 1986, killing all seven crew members.

Launch and recovery are the most critical parts of a manned flight, although careful supervision is needed at all times. With extended tours there is the added risk of bodily deterioration under low gravity or weightless conditions – this is countered by regular exercise programmes.

Manned rockets

Soviet *Soyuz* capsules are rocket-launched three-person vehicles used to ferry cosmonauts to and from the *Salyut* and *Mir* space stations. Recovery from orbit starts with an engine burn to reduce orbital speed, and separation of the orbital and instrument modules, which burn up. As the manned capsule falls into the atmosphere, a heat-resisting shield absorbs the heat generated by friction with the atmosphere. The main recovery parachute opens at a height of about 10 km (6 miles), the heat shield is discarded and retro-rockets are fired to cushion the landing.

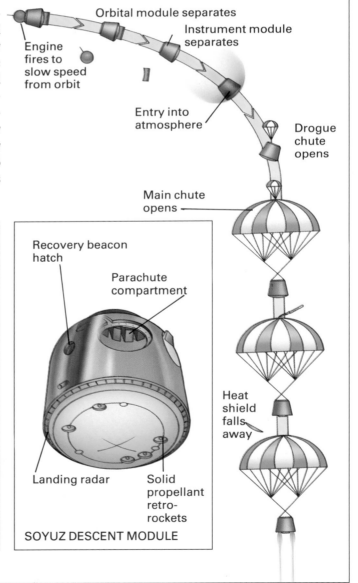

Orbital module separates

Instrument module separates

Engine fires to slow speed from orbit

Entry into atmosphere

Drogue chute opens

Main chute opens

Recovery beacon hatch

Parachute compartment

Landing radar

Solid propellant retro-rockets

Heat shield falls away

SOYUZ DESCENT MODULE

The Soviet *MIR* space station

Rockets to the planets

Journeys to the other planets of the Solar System are carried out by boosting the spacecraft to speed and letting it coast to its destination following an elliptical orbit. Where possible, probes are launched when the relative positions of the planets give the shortest travel time.

A manned round trip to Mars would take around two years, depending on the planetary alignment. American plans for such a trip were originally based on the use of a nuclear engine producing a thrust of 90,700 kg (200,000 lb). In the Nerva engine, hydrogen is pumped through the core of a nuclear reactor to give a hot, high-speed jet. This design avoids the need to carry large amounts of oxidant as well as the fuel. However, more recent flight plans are based on the use of conventional liquid-fuel rocket engines.

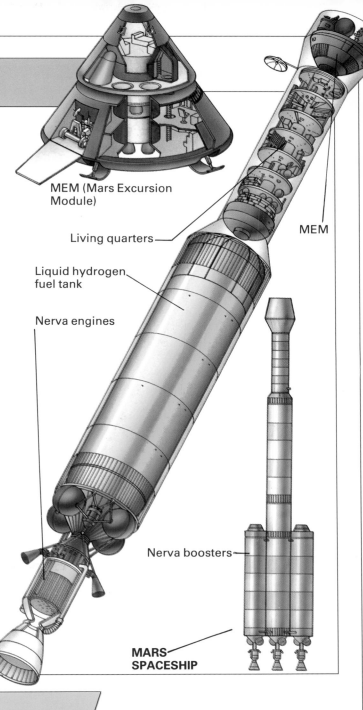

MEM (Mars Excursion Module)

Living quarters

Liquid hydrogen fuel tank

Nerva engines

Nerva boosters

MEM

MARS SPACESHIP

A solar-powered probe to Venus

Rockets to the stars

Using existing rockets, it would take several hundred thousand years to reach even the nearest star, Proxima Centauri, which is 25 trillion miles away. Interstellar travel will need new types of rockets which can provide sustained thrust. One possibility is the Orion concept, which would use a series of nuclear explosions to give drive pulses.

However, some spacecraft are already on their way out into space. The *Pioneer 10* and *11* probes have completed their fly-pasts of Jupiter and Saturn, and are now heading out of the solar system at speeds of over 186 million mi/year.

The *Pioneer 11* space probe flies past Saturn.

29

MOTIVE POWER IN THE AIR

Rolls Royce Merlin V-12 piston engines produced up to 2,640 hp from their 27 liters.

Frank Whittle's jet engine first ran in 1937, and in 1941 flew in a Gloster test aircraft.

The Pratt & Whitney PW4060 turbofan has 60,000 lb thrust.

Improvements in aircraft speed, range and reliability have depended on the development of suitable power plants. Gas turbine engines – commonly called jets – are the main power sources for modern aircraft, either producing direct jet thrust or driving propellers or turbofans. The engine built by the Wright brothers for their first flight produced just 12 hp. Modern jet engines are rated by the thrust they produce. Each Rolls Royce RB211B on a Boeing 747 has a thrust of 54,000 lb, which is the equivalent of an output of more than 20,000 hp.

Propeller blades have an airfoil shape that generates a forward pull as the propeller turns, and accelerates the air backward to give thrust. With variable pitch propellers, the angle the blades make with the air can be changed from fine, to give maximum thrust at take-off, to coarse, for cruising flight. Reverse pitch produces a forward thrust for braking after landing.

Propeller efficiency falls off at high speeds as the blade tips start to approach the speed of sound. Because of this propellers are usually used for flight speeds below 500 mph.

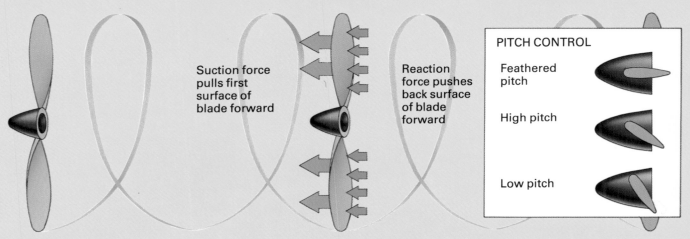

Suction force pulls first surface of blade forward

Reaction force pushes back surface of blade forward

PITCH CONTROL

Feathered pitch

High pitch

Low pitch

Piston engines are widely used for comparatively slow-speed light aircraft, with models like the Avco *Lycoming* IO-720 having outputs up to 400 hp. The Porsche PFM 3200 was developed from the 911S sports car engine, and is a 3.2 liter air-cooled design with six opposed cylinders. It is a compact and lightweight design with a power output of 210 hp.

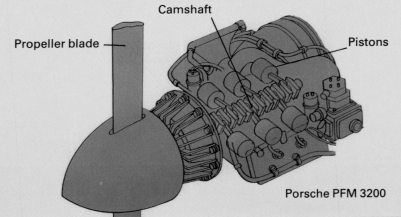

Camshaft

Propeller blade

Pistons

Porsche PFM 3200

Turbojet

Turbojets are the simplest type of gas turbine. All the air passes through the combustion chamber, giving a high-velocity jet best suited to supersonic aircraft.

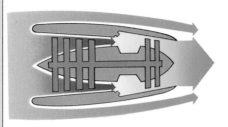

Turbojet

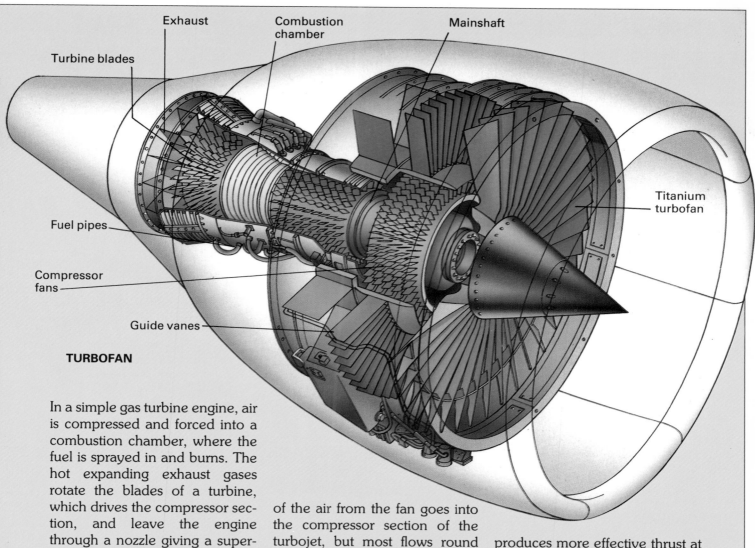

Turbine blades
Exhaust
Combustion chamber
Mainshaft

Fuel pipes

Compressor fans

Guide vanes

Titanium turbofan

TURBOFAN

In a simple gas turbine engine, air is compressed and forced into a combustion chamber, where the fuel is sprayed in and burns. The hot expanding exhaust gases rotate the blades of a turbine, which drives the compressor section, and leave the engine through a nozzle giving a supersonic jet.

High bypass jet engines have a turbojet core, with an extra turbine section that drives a large diameter fan at the front. Some of the air from the fan goes into the compressor section of the turbojet, but most flows round the outside of the core engine. The bypass airflow is combined with the jet from the core engine. This gives a much larger mass of air moving at a slower speed, and produces more effective thrust at subsonic aircraft speeds. Turbofans combine the power of the turbojet with the fuel efficiency and low noise levels of propeller engines.

Turbofan
Turbofans are reliable and fuel-efficient. They are often produced as families – Rolls Royce's RB211 series has thrusts from 37,400 lb to 74,000 lb.

Turboprop
In turboprop engines, power from the turbine drives a front-mounted propeller through a gearbox. They are most suitable for speeds up to 800 km/h (500 mph).

Propfan
Jet prop engines have curved-blade propellers that are efficient at aircraft speeds up to 1,000 km/h (620 mph).

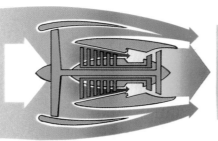

Turbofan

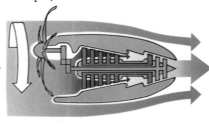

Turboprop

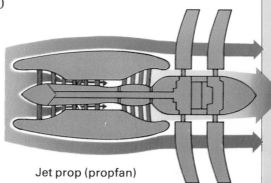

Jet prop (propfan)

ROCKET POWER

Gunpowder rockets were used by the Chinese in the 11th century.

Robert Goddard launched the first liquid fuel rocket in 1926. Using gasoline and oxygen, it flew 56 m (114 ft),

Most engines use oxygen from the air to burn their fuel. But rockets get their oxygen from an oxidant carried in addition to the fuel. As a result, rockets can operate high in the atmosphere and out in space, where there is no air.

Solid fuel rockets have the fuel and oxidant (to supply oxygen) combined to give a propellant which is packed into the rocket's body. Once lit, the propellant burns until it is all used up. Liquid fuel rockets have separate fuel and oxidant. They are pumped from storage tanks into the rocket engine.

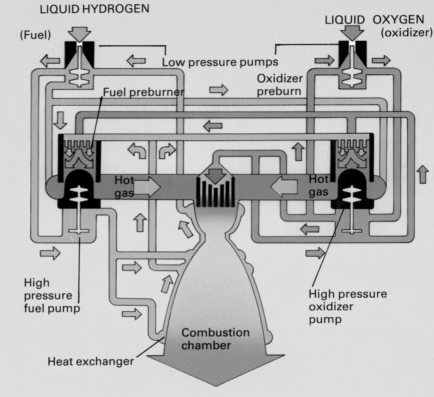

LIQUID HYDROGEN (Fuel)

LIQUID OXYGEN (oxidizer)

Low pressure pumps

Fuel preburner

Oxidizer preburn

Hot gas

Hot gas

High pressure fuel pump

High pressure oxidizer pump

Combustion chamber

Heat exchanger

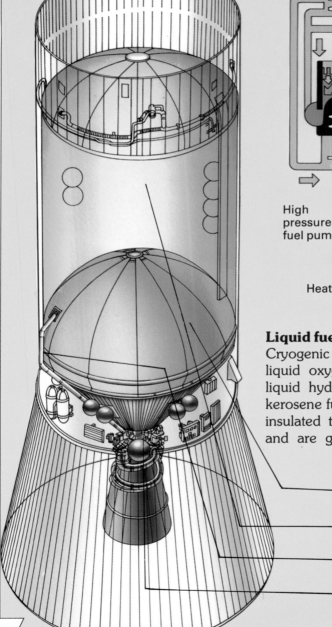

Liquid oxygen

Liquid hydrogen

Fuel line

Gimbal engine mountings

Liquid fuel rockets

Cryogenic rocket engines use liquid oxygen (at -147°C) with liquid hydrogen (at -251°C) or kerosene fuel. The tanks are well insulated to keep the fuel cold and are generally filled shortly before launch. Other liquid propellants such as UDMH (unsymmetrical dimethylhydrazine) and nitrogen tetroxide can be held in the rocket fuel tanks for extended periods.

Turbopumps – driven by gases from preburners – feed fuel to the combustion chamber. Some of it circulates round the outside of the combustion chamber and nozzle to keep it cool. In the Shuttle engine the chamber wall is kept below 600°C, although the combustion temperature is about 3,300°C. The nozzle can be angled to direct the thrust.

Small rocket engines using liquid fuel and oxidant are fitted to spacecraft and satellites for controlling their position in space. Single-liquid propellants, called monopropellants, such as hydrazine and hydrogen peroxide are also used. They decompose over a catalyst to produce a stream of hot gas. The limited amount of space for the storage of fuel for these control rockets is a major restriction on the working lives of low-orbit satellites.

Stored gas is used for propulsion in the Shuttle Manned Maneuvering Unit (MMU). This has a total of 24 small jets supplied from two tanks holding 11.9 kg (26 lb) of nitrogen. Hand controllers operate groups of jets for the required movement.

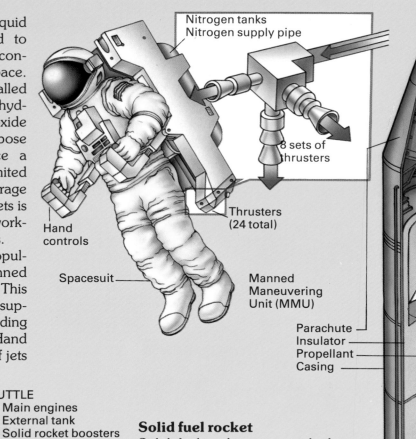

Nitrogen tanks
Nitrogen supply pipe
8 sets of thrusters
Thrusters (24 total)
Hand controls
Spacesuit
Manned Maneuvering Unit (MMU)

Parachute
Insulator
Propellant
Casing

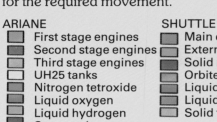

ARIANE		SHUTTLE	
	First stage engines		Main engines
	Second stage engines		External tank
	Third stage engines		Solid rocket boosters
	UH25 tanks		Orbiter fuel
	Nitrogen tetroxide		Liquid oxygen
	Liquid oxygen		Liquid hydrogen
	Liquid hydrogen		Solid fuel
	Strap-on boosters		

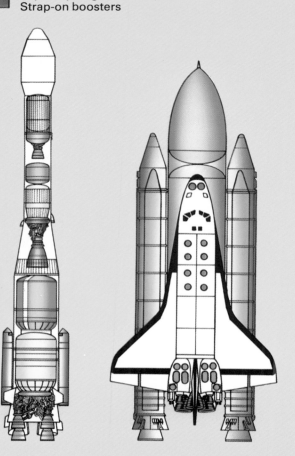

Solid fuel rocket

Solid fuel rockets are ready for immediate firing and are widely used for missiles. Another important application is as boosters for space launchers. The booster rockets for the space shuttle use aluminum perchlorate oxidizer and aluminum powder fuel. Iron oxide is used as a catalyst to control combustion and the materials are held together by a plastic binder, which also acts as fuel. Each rocket weighs 589.67 tons and has a lift-off thrust of 1,497 tons. The propellant charges are shaped to give a reduced thrust later in the flight.

After their 127-second burn, the booster rockets are freed from the main tank by an explosive system, and the separation motors are fired to push the rockets away from the tank and orbiter. The rockets continue in a ballistic trajectory and fall back to Earth. The final descent is slowed by a set of three parachutes and the rockets splash down into the ocean about 250 km (160 miles) down range from the launch site.

Designers and pilots have been trying to prove that their aircraft are the fastest or can fly farthest since soon after flying began.

Formal trials like the Schnieder Trophy competitions for seaplanes had a definite effect in refining designs and increasing aircraft performance. Similarly, pioneering flights often laid the foundations for regular services. The pressures of two World Wars, followed by the Cold War, also had a marked effect on performance.

Speed records and height records are generally given for aircraft that take off under their own power.

Higher speeds and greater heights are achieved with aircraft carried into the air by a motherplane and released at height to make their flight.

There have been many attempts to conquer space, and the space race between the USA and the USSR reached its peak in the 1960s and 1970s. Recently the huge cost of exploring space has caused a slowdown in the race.

Early manned space flights lasted only a few hours. This time was gradually extended to days, and astronauts can now remain in space for periods of up to a year without significant problems.

AIR RECORDS

First controlled flight: Orville and Wilbur Wright (USA), 36.5 m (120 ft) lasting 12 sec, 1903.

First crossing of the English Channel: Louis Blériot (France), in his *Blériot XI*, lasting 36½ min, 1909.

First non-stop crossing of the Atlantic: Capt John Alcock and Lt Arthur Brown (UK), in a Vickers *Vimy*, 1919.

First non-stop solo crosing of the Atlantic: Capt Charles Lindbergh (USA), in the *Spirit of St Louis*, 1927.

First non-stop crossing of the Pacific: Major Clyde Pangborn and Hugh Herndon (USA), in *Miss Veedol*, 1931.

First supersonic scheduled passenger flight: *Concorde* (UK and France), 1976.

Official air speed record: 3529.56 km/h (2193.167mph) by Capt Eldon Joersz and Maj George Morgan (USA), in a *Lockheed* SR-71A, 1976.

Official world altitude record by aircraft taking off from ground: 37.650 m (123.524 ft) by Alexander Fedotov (USSR), in a MIG-25, 1977.

First round-the-world flight without refuelling: Dick Rutan and Jeana Yeager (USA), in *Voyager*, 1986.

The long distance record-holder, *Voyager*

SPACE RECORDS

First war rockets: Propelled by gun-powder these were used in China and first detailed in 1042.

First true, modern rocket: Germany launches V2 against England, 1944.

The world's first satellite: The Soviet Union launches *Sputnik 1* 1957.

The first man in space: Lt Yuri Gagarin (USSR) completes one orbit of the Earth, 1961.

The first communications satellite: *Telstar*, (USA), 1962.

The first woman in space: Valentina Tereshkova (USSR), 1963.

The first space walk: Alexi Leonov (USSR), 1965.

First man on the Moon: *Apollo II* (USA) launched on lunar landing mission. Neil Armstrong becomes first man to set foot on Moon, 1969.

First probe to Jupiter, Saturn and Uranus: *Voyager 2* (USA), 1977.

First flight of Space Shuttle: *Columbia* (USA), 1981.

Longest manned space flight: Vladimir Titov and Musa Manarov (USSR), spent 365 days on the *MIR* space station.

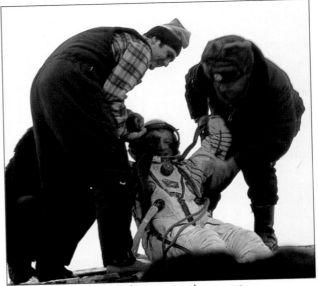

Soviet cosmonaut after a year in space

GLOSSARY

ablative material that protects a surface from excessive heat, as on a spacecraft during re-entry.

aerodynamics study of the movement of air and other gases and of the forces on bodies when they move relative to the gases.

aileron hinged rear section on an aircraft wing. Ailerons on each wing are moved in opposite directions to give roll.

airfoil body shaped so its movement relative to a gas produces a force (lift) perpendicular to the motion.

airship lighter-than-air aircraft with a means of propulsion and directional control.

apogee point on a satellite orbit that is farthest from the Earth.

ballistics study of the motion of projectiles.

booster secondary rocket fitted to a launch vehicle.

convertiplanes heavier-than-air aircraft that use rotors to take off (like a helicopter) and then convert to a fixed-wing operation for normal flight.

cryogenic describing temperatures below -195.6°C (-320.08°F), the boiling point of liquid nitrogen.

elevator hinged rear part of an aircraft's tailplane, used to give the aircraft pitch movements.

escape velocity speed needed for an object to escape from gravitational attraction. For the surface of the Earth, it is 11.2 km/s (6.95 miles/sec) and for the Moon, 2.4 km/s (1.5 miles/sec).

flaps hinged control surfaces on a wing.

hypersonic speed greater than five times the speed of sound.

lift component of aerodynamic force produced by the airflow over a body (such as a wing) and acting perpendicular to the undisturbed airflow.

Mach number ratio of the speed of an aircraft (or other object) to the local speed of sound. The speed of sound in air depends on temperature – it is lower at high altitudes where the air is colder. It varies from about 1225 km/h (760 mph) in warm air at sea level, to about 1060 kmh (660 mph) at great heights.

microlight small powered aircraft with an unladen weight less than 150 kg (330 lb).

monopropellant rocket propellant that can produce thrust without needing the addition of a second substance.

NASA National Aeronautics and Space Administration, the American organization responsible for space activities.

payload extra load that can be carried, beyond that needed by an aircraft or rocket for its operation.

perigee point on a satellite orbit that is nearest to the Earth.

propellant mixture of fuel and oxidizer burned in a rocket engine to produce thrust.

retrorockets rockets fired to slow down the movement of a space vehicle.

rocket jet propulsion engine that uses its own supplies of fuel and oxidant.

satellite object in orbit around another body. Generally describes an artificial satellite launched by a rocket.

slot air gap formed between a wing and a secondary airfoil or flap. Air flowing through the slot is directed over the wing surface and delays the onset of stall.

speed of sound see mach

stall breakaway of airflow from an airfoil causing a sudden loss of lift.

STOL short take-off and landing.

strategic missile missile used to attack the home territory and industrial base of an enemy. Generally with thermonuclear warheads.

supersonic speed greater than the speed of sound.

tactical missile missile used for tactical purposes, to attack an enemy's forces in the course of a battle. It may have conventional or nuclear explosive warheads, or carry chemical weapons.

thermal related to temperature.

trajectory path described by an object, such as a shell or rocket, moving through space.

ultralight see microlight.

VTOL vertical take-off and landing.

warhead section of a missile containing the chemical or nuclear explosive charge.

INDEX

Photographic Credits:
t=top, b=bottom, m=middle, l=left, r=right
Cover: NASA; page 3: Zefa; pages 5, 6, 12b, 13t, 15
and 19: Robert Harding Library; page 7: Airbus Industries;
pages 9, 10, 13b, 20 and 21: Salamander Books; pages
11l and 34b: Frank Spooner Agency; pages 11r, 12t 27
and back cover: Daily Telegraph Colour Library; page 14
The Research House; page 23: European Space Agency;
pages 29t and 34t: Rex Features; page 29b: Science
Photo Library.